IMAGES
of America

RESIDENTIAL
ARCHITECTURE
IN THE EAST BAY

IMAGES
of America

RESIDENTIAL ARCHITECTURE IN THE EAST BAY

Jennifer Joey McCallon

ARCADIA
PUBLISHING

Published by Arcadia Publishing
Charleston, South Carolina

Printed in the United States of America

Library of Congress Control Number: 2023941588

For all general information, please contact Arcadia Publishing:
Telephone 843-853-2070
Fax 843-853-0044
E-mail sales@arcadiapublishing.com

Visit us on the Internet at www.arcadiapublishing.com

Much gratitude to my children (Elo, Milo, and Lil), my husband (Brett), everyone I work with at Keller Williams Realty, and all my friends for their support

CONTENTS

ACKNOWLEDGMENTS

Being a real estate broker, living in Oakland and later Alameda, has been incredibly inspirational. I suspect my own home is from some sort of plan book, but it is impossible to know for sure. Like many homes, it has been renovated too many times to know what was really going on here in the first place—a new foundation and an upper floor were added sometime in the middle of the century.

I hope you enjoy this book, inspired during the pandemic and put off for months after we started getting out and about again.

Much gratitude to the Richmond Museum, Albany Library, and San Leandro Library for all their help with putting this book together. Additional appreciation is extended to my children (Elo, Milo and Lil) and my husband (Brett), everyone I work with at Keller Williams, my clients, friends, and neighbors who were all so supportive in finishing this project.

INTRODUCTION

Residential architecture in the East Bay is as varied as its diverse population—and while similar in design and features to homes in the rest of the country and even other parts of California, Bay Area houses have a certain uniqueness that cannot quite be defined.

Many East Bay cities and towns came of age in the first part of the 20th century, with spikes in increased population caused by events outside of the East Bay. For the purpose of this book, we are going to focus exclusively on the inner East Bay, from Richmond to the north, to Alameda and San Leandro, and inland only as far as Oakland.

Starting with the great earthquake and fire of 1906, followed by the world war, there were upticks in housing developments in the inner East Bay. This book surveys the incredibly varied styles of homes in the East Bay that were built over the first part of the 20th century, from the few early cabins, cottages, and worker homes of the 1900s–1920s to the Craftsman, catalog, and plan book homes from the 1910s–1940s, to the war housing the sprouted up during World War II in Richmond and all the way down to Alameda along the Bay coast and how that was converted to postwar housing.

This book is not intended to be an exhaustive sampling of East Bay housing styles, as there are far more than could be covered here, and I was limited to the available resources from local collections, public and private.

The East Bay had many influential architects, including Bernard Ralph Maybeck, an instructor at the University of California, Berkeley, and highly influential in the Arts and Crafts movement of the early 20th century, a style that many builders, developers, and plan books emulated. Julia Morgan was, in 1904, the first woman to obtain an architecture license in California and she was the unofficial principal architect for Mills College. Lilian Bridgeman built design-forward homes that would influence architecture for decades to come. Paul Williams was a well-known African American California architect who lived and practiced primarily in Los Angeles; his books, however, *The Small Home of Tomorrow* and *New Homes for Today*, were very influential in the building styles of the East Bay. There are many mid-century architects, but the most well-known is Joseph Eichler, who was not actually an architect by trade, but rather a builder that came to be known for his unique style.

If you've traveled much around the United States, you've probably noticed different building materials in different areas, as it makes sense to build with what you have—red or yellow bricks in the Midwest and South, wood in some places, stone in others, shingle siding in others. In the East Bay, an area prone to earthquakes, most homes are built of wood framing with stucco exteriors. There are also some wood-paneled homes and shingle homes as well. During the first half of the 20th century, the wood was sourced from its very own redwood forests, which makes for a sturdy, long-lasting home.

Racial discrimination and segregation were a critical part of the development of neighborhoods in the East Bay. "Redlining" prevailed all over the United States, and the East Bay area was not immune to the cultural influences of America. Systematic housing discrimination during the 20th century is rooted in government discrimination brought about by the New Deal. In order to assist homeowners who were defaulting on mortgages due to economic hardship caused by the Depression, the Home Owners Loan Corporation (HOLC) was created to offer more affordable mortgages. As a part of this plan, the agency created maps of major cities throughout the United States in the second half of the 1930s.

HOLC provided not only color-coded maps, but descriptions of inhabitants, be they Italians, new immigrants, Asians, or Black Americans, and considered the value of the land to be based on the races and ethnicities of the people who lived there. All white areas were highly regarded with mixed populations coming in lower and all-Black areas the riskiest for lending, making home ownership in Black neighborhoods increasingly difficult for the population and increasing the number of renters in those areas. It decreased new development and discouraged home ownership. This type guided the lending practices of cities large and small across the United States for decades. The homes that were built in the 1920s were inaccessible to all; this is an important point to remember as we look at the architectural features of these houses.

One

OAKLAND

Oakland's many neighborhoods are as diverse as its people. For the purpose of this book, the photographs are limited to what the author was able to procure, which display a few selected areas: the Fruitvale and lower Dimond, a little bit of Rockridge, a bit of Maxwell Park, and a few other favorite homes.

When Oakland was founded, its original boundaries were just south of the intersections of Broadway, Fourteenth Street, and San Pablo Avenue. Later, farmland and towns to the east and north were gradually acquired by the metropolis. Oakland's growing industrial importance and the necessity for sea access led to the dredging of a shipping and tidal channel in 1902. This created what is now the well-known and charming island of the adjacent town of Alameda. Oakland was on its way to growing into a big city when the earthquake and fire in San Francisco happened in 1900. About 400,000 people were displaced and became part of the massive influx of refugees that moved to the sunny side of the Bay.

Oakland was by and large developed in the early 20th century, and thousands of permanent homes were built right after World War I. As stated in a pamphlet marketing the Fruitvale District from that era, one could always hear the sound of hammers and saws, with homes going up in record numbers. Many neighborhoods, including the Bancroft District and Maxwell Park, were developed as private, race-restricted neighborhoods restricted with covenants in place demanding that only those of European descent live there. Maxwell Park, for example, was founded in the early 1920s as a private Whites-only neighborhood, "restricted as to Orientals, Asiatics, and Africans." Purchased by John P. Maxwell, a native of Illinois and later a resident of Adams Point, the development was advertised as "Oakland's Addition Beautiful."

The most prevalent styles of home in Oakland were the Craftsman and bungalow, with some mass-produced and others from catalogs and plan books.

Craftsman homes tend to have personality in every room, encouraging one to sit and socialize on its strong, covered front porch. Craftsman homes have a few central design aspects including a covered front porch, tapered columns supporting the porch, roof eaves that overhang and are exposed, and a low-pitched gable roof. A bungalow-style home can include these aspects; however, they are usually a little simpler in design and single-level.

Designers in this era wanted to move away from the cluttered look of Victorian homes. Craftsman homes appeared fresh and modern; simple clean lines on a home's exterior walls were a refreshing change from all the Victorian trim, frills, scrolls, and embellishments. It makes sense for Oakland to be home to so many Craftsman houses being that so much building was done in Oakland during the Craftsman era.

This small booklet filled with colorful illustrations and photographs advertised the Fruitvale District on behalf of local developers, attempting to draw a new population to this sunny alternative to San Francisco. The Fruitvale District was flat and warm compared to the cold hills and fog of San Francisco. "The following description of the FRUITVALE, CAL., as presented to the reader, is a conservative statement of its wonderful advantages." (Courtesy Oakland History Room, Oakland Public Library.)

In Fruitvale, California, the "Right sort of people live here." The Fruitvale was exactly that—a vale of fruits, or a neighborhood of fruit trees. The infrastructure of a sanitary system was built in, and the lots were ready for building. This Fruitvale postcard advertises the Fruitvale to San Franciscans with directions on how to get there on the ferry steamer. (Courtesy Oakland History Room, Oakland Public Library.)

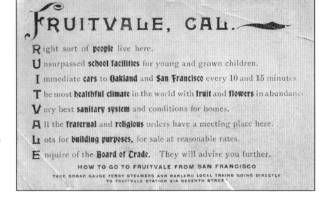

"The climate is warm and delightful. No bitter blasts or dense fogs every mar the pleasure of the dweller in this sheltered nook . . . here flourish fruits and flowers in almost tropical luxuriance." The description of the Fruitvale District is one of "tropical luxuriance"—not necessarily what is thought of in Oakland today. (Courtesy Oakland History Room, Oakland Public Library.)

This modest Victorian home has ornate features, including a decorative roofline, a complex roofing structure with both pyramid and hip roof styles, carved wood over the front windows, and a fanciful pitched roof over the porch. Note the decorative pitched roof, double French doors, and additional decorations along the roofline. (Courtesy Oakland History Room, Oakland Public Library.)

"Coby Home" on Sixteenth Street in Fruitvale featured wood siding (this was often replaced later in the 20th century with stucco, which added protection as well as a level of insulation), leaded glass windows, and a delicate Juliet balcony. The photograph states it is on Sixteenth Street, which one can guess was later changed to E. Sixteenth Street. A laundromat is now located at that address. (Courtesy Oakland History Room, Oakland Public Library.)

SPACIOUS RESIDENCE IN UPPER FRUITVALE

The Fruitvale District was known for spacious, elegant homes in the first half of the 20th century. Eighteenth Street was lined with large, luxurious homes that were an alternative to the more-crowded San Francisco homes that people left following the earthquake and fire. The East Bay was warm and welcoming, with lovely architectural details and tree-lined streets. (Courtesy Oakland History Room, Oakland Public Library.)

Not all homes in the Fruitvale District were spacious and elegant. This modest home with a windowless dormer pop-out shows some wear and tear in its edges and signs of decay. Note the more basic columns that hold the roof up and the lack of decorative features. A rickety picket fence stretches across the front yard. A woman standing behind the fence wears a modest dress and pinafore. There are no power lines going to the house. (Courtesy Oakland History Room, Oakland Public Library.)

BEAUTIFUL RESIDENCE ON FRUITVALE AVENUE

This incredibly ornate small mansion on Fruitvale Avenue set back from the street features a broad lawn and manicured shrubbery. It has a combination of many styles including Roman Tuscan columns, a complex roofing system, a covered wraparound porch, ornate arched windows, and decorative eaves. A decorative style such as this indicates prosperity and taste. (Courtesy Oakland History Room, Oakland Public Library.)

Building and Improvement.

The trees and shrubs form a dainty, fragrant screen over every window, door and veranda, and one forgets that man has builded here, so lost is he in admiration of the profusion of flowers and trees.

The sound of the hammer and saw has not ceased summer or winter, and still the good work continues. Stately mansions and artistic cottages are building in every direction. Enterprising men, seeing the great opportunity for trade, are making haste to meet its demands, and the corner of East Fourteenth Street and Fruitvale Avenue is rapidly growing into a thriving business center. Here has just been completed a large two-story business block adjoining the postoffice. Fruitvale Avenue for a distance of about two miles is lined with picturesque and elegant homes in the center of well-kept, spacious grounds. Looking to the east and west, the eye is not disappointed; each home betokens thrift and comfort.

This brochure states, "The sound of the hammer and saw has not ceased summer or winter, and still the good work continues. Stately mansions and artistic cottages are building in every direction." The brochure further explains, "Looking to the east and west, the eye is not disappointed; each home betokens thrift and comfort." (Courtesy Oakland History Room, Oakland Public Library.)

This home was raised to make room for a full basement later on in the 20th century. It is a classic bungalow with some Craftsman features and a hint of Edwardian charm. The little faux balcony below the windows is a unique decorative feature. The eaves, in the Craftsman style, are open and exposed. (Courtesy Liz Bachen.)

Seen here is the School Street house, which was raised later in the 20th century to add a full lower level. The decorative balcony-like structure was removed, and the windows have been replaced. A garage was added to accommodate the resident's car. Delicate scalloping remains above the window on the right-hand side. (Courtesy Liz Bachen.)

A man inside the house on School Street is holding his saxophone, standing on a highly decorative carpet or possibly oilcloth floor next to an incredibly opulent piano adorned with a large vase of flowers. There is no shortage among the resident owners of house pride in this lovely modest home on School Street. (Courtesy Liz Bachen.)

The dining room decor was sparse and tidy in the interior of this 1920s Fruitvale home. Note the dark hardwood floors, a stone fireplace, and a small table. Built-in shelving is there to accommodate dining necessities. A photograph sits on the mantle. A bright but delicate lamp hangs from the ceiling. A window seat runs the length of the large picture window. (Courtesy Liz Bachen.)

The original owners of Fruitvale House are pictured here in front of some shrubbery on School Street in the late 1960s. On the left is the youngest daughter, Phyllis, and the younger woman on her right is her niece by marriage. Interestingly, Phyllis's husband, Toye, who was a musician in another photograph, was known in the area as the lead flutist for the Bohemian Club. (Courtesy Liz Bachen.)

After the house was lifted, the owner used the basement as a hobby space where he would collect various photographs from magazines and decoupage them on the walls. The current owners have maintained this decor. The images range from decorative calendars, sports legends, and architectural marvels to wonders of the world and nature scenes. (Courtesy Liz Bachen.)

A family stands outside a fine shingle home with a pyramid roof, dormer windows, and exposed eaves. The windows have shades and awnings to keep the heat out. A home was a source of pride and a place to socialize and rest. There is a telephone or electrical pole. The family sits in its fine automobile with a small windmill in the backyard. (Courtesy Oakland History Room, Oakland Public Library.)

Here is a map of the Maxwell Park neighborhood of Oakland. Homes were built rapidly during the years following World War I. The map states that Maxwell Park is "the only new addition to be put on the market this year that will have all the improvements in, ready to build." It also claims that "the property is restricted as to Orientals, Asiatics and Africans." (Courtesy the Bancroft Library.)

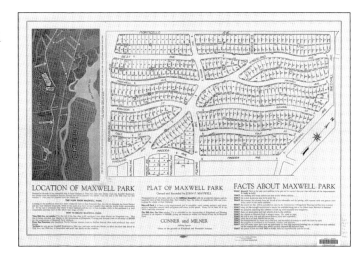

Pictured are Maxwell Park Homes with plenty of bold-colored and striped awnings with scalloped edges. This home also features a low-pitched roof and plenty of landscaping, shrubbery, and a green lawn. The windows are wood framed, and the fireplace is off to the side. The porch is covered and integrated into the rectangular footprint of the home. (Courtesy Oakland History Center.)

"Maxwell Park Becomes 'Little Piedmont' in Two Years." This article states that "Maxwell Park has become a home tract of established and increasing value. More than 300 homes have been completed or are in course of construction. The 55th Avenue car line has been extended into the center of the park giving quick and frequent transportation to the heart of Oakland, with the Southern Pacific's Ferry service within walking distance. All improvements of the finest character have been installed." This appeared in the *Oakland Tribune* on May 19, 1923.

Here is a view of Maxwell Park Homes for sale and the Burritt & Shealy Office. Note the wide variety of home styles with varying roof lines, styles, and sizes. All the houses appear to have stairs to their backyards and consistent setbacks from the street. Power lines stretch from utility poles, bringing modern amenities to these new homes. (Courtesy Oakland History Center.)

This advertisement for Knowles Porter and Young exclaims, "FOR SALE! Beautiful New Central Bungalow Complete in every detail. Excellent Location and Priced Right!" These were part of the original tract housing movement that started in the 1920s. The lack of decorative elements and streamlined roofs was an intentional pivot from the highly decorative Victorians of an earlier era. (Courtesy Oakland History Center.)

This row of homes on a gently upslope curving street with small uncovered porches shows different types of rooflines, including one double-V type right at the start of the row. Space for trees along with a sidewalk and little walkways take one to each new front door. Telephone and electrical poles bring modern necessities to each home. (Courtesy Oakland History Center.)

Here, homes are being built on a curved upslope street. The utility poles have been placed, but there are no power lines. Houses are mass-produced in rows to provide shelter for the rapidly growing population in Oakland. These are classic "stick built" structures. They are generally drafted by an architect, which the client then approves. The building is subsequently erected after the materials are brought to the job site. (Courtesy Oakland History Center.)

This advertisement for Burritt & Shealey states, "Thousands of Oakland men and women are considering the purchase of a home." They are "wishing for one, but getting nowhere. They pay the rent on a home every month, but acquire no equity in it. They make money, but accumulate nothing. They help the city prosper and do not share in that prosperity for the reason that they lack the wisdom and initiative to step out and 'pick' theirs while the 'Picking' is possible." This ad appeared in the *Oakland Tribune* on May 27, 1923.

Well-trained horses help workers build Maxwell Park. In the background, one can see a variety of uniquely Maxwell Park houses along the rolling slopes with architectural features, including varied facades, upslope and downslope homes, arched doorways, covered porches, small uncovered porches, as well as Mission-style, Spanish-style, and Craftsman-style homes, all lined up in perfect harmony. (Courtesy Oakland History Center.)

Homes are going up in Maxwell Park. Developers worked quickly to build new homes to meet the demand of a growing population. Redwood lumber rests on newly constructed city streets. Pitched roofs wait to be assembled, and many of the homes have detached garages waiting for cars at the end of long driveways, while the homes quietly await new owners. (Courtesy Oakland History Center.)

Split-level homes are being built in Maxwell Park in the 1920s. This type of split-level style was popular all over the East Bay. These homes feature redwood framing (which would be covered in stucco upon completion), pitched roofs, and exposed eaves and are nearly identical to each other in a tidy row along a tree-lined street. (Courtesy Oakland History Center.)

Here is a unique Spanish-style Craftsman in Maxwell Park. Built in 1921, this home features an arched entry, a pop-out window, and a flat roof. Like many, the home is built on a slope with a full basement below. Decorative features adorn the front exterior, including shutters, tiles, and scalloped metal detail along the roof line. (Photograph by the author.)

Pictured is a classic Maxwell Park home with a Spanish tiled roof, a modest covered porch that cuts into the footprint of the home, an arched window, and a brick chimney. Wide stairs lead to the entryway with metal railings. Clay-tiled roofing systems such as the one on this house have been around for hundreds of years. Archeologists have recovered specimens of clay roofing tiles from the 1585 settlement of Roanoke Island in North Carolina. (Photograph by the author.)

Robert C. Hillen created this subdivision of "modest mansions" on Picardy Drive. This home features a rounded turret on the left with storybook styling. Each home in this small subdivision is slightly different from the next; some had crenelated parapets among other variations in the roof lines. Some have arched windows, others are built with rectangular windows and wooden beams, similar to a Tudor style. All have storybook charm. (Photograph by the author.)

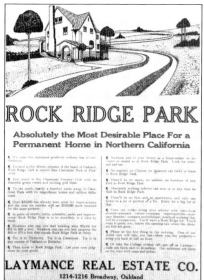

Today, we think of Oakland as diverse and open to everyone. This was not always the case. As homes popped up all over Oakland, they were often designed with specific demographics in mind. This advertisement for Layman Real Estate states that "no negroes, no Chinese, no Japanese can build in Rock Ridge Park." It further notes that "there'll be no stores, no saloons, no business of any kind in Rock Ridge Park." And of course, there will also be "no flats and no apartments, and only one house to a lot or portion of a lot." (Courtesy Oakland History Room, Oakland Public Library.)

This is a perfect and beautifully designed example of a shingled Craftsman home with a double front-gabled roof. This sweet home features a covered porch, a shingled exterior, and a window in the attic. Attic space was generally unfinished and inaccessible, so the windows were strictly decorative. Note the curled detailing along the roofline. Brick knee walls surround the porch; these short walls, typically around three feet high, allowed homeowners to sit on the porch and see out into the world while providing privacy and a certain architectural look and feel. (Photograph by the author.)

Seen here is a Rockridge home with a side gabled roof and large dormer window. It has a fully covered porch with long exposed beams. Square pillars support the roof of the house. Most likely built in the 1910s, this home has three large windows across the front along what appears to be a bay window, with a window bench in the interior. (Photograph by the author.)

Fancy curled detailing on the dormer roof gives this home a little extra something special. This added bit of flare appears on Craftsman homes in different neighborhoods around the East Bay. Wide tapered columns support the roof over the covered porch. A large window in the front may have been a single window instead of three when the home was originally built. (Photograph by the author.)

As Oakland expanded, stately homes were built along Mandana Boulevard in the East Piedmont tract of the Trestle Glen District of Oakland. These homes were spacious and gracious Foursquare-style homes without the porches featured on smaller Craftsman's being built at the same time. It could be deduced that for the wealthy, it was less appealing to socialize in front of one's home. (Courtesy Oakland History Room, Oakland Public Library.)

Two

SAN LEANDRO

San Leandro was a bustling small town in the 1840s when forty-niners arrived and ignored the title claims of the Spanish who had lived there for decades (and the Spanish had, of course, ignored the claims of the Ohlone natives who were there before them). The first trolley cars made their way to San Leandro in 1892, and in 1898 telephone service was established. Streetlights appeared, and homes were being built at a relatively rapid pace. San Leandro remained a primarily rural community until 1935 when, to quicken economic recovery from the Great Depression, Pres. Franklin Delano Roosevelt launched the New Deal in 1934. Programs aimed to boost homeownership provided mortgage insurance and funded the construction of new suburban neighborhoods. Redlining resulted from those mortgage loans, which were provided through the Federal Housing Act (FHA), typically exclusively going to white homebuyers. Furthermore, racial covenants, conditions, and limitations resulted from the federal financial assistance provided to developments during this period with the stipulation that the properties could not be sold to Black homebuyers. Therefore, despite the fact that these initiatives boosted the economy, they also led to government-supported housing segregation.

Today, redlining is a general term referring to racism in housing. The phrase is derived from maps that the federal government produced in 1934 for 142 urban centers across the nation to determine where it was "safe" to insure mortgages; areas of cities were color-coded. The color red represented the places deemed to be too dangerous for mortgage loan insurance. Areas that are good candidates for house loans (often the newer, white communities) were highlighted in green. A neighborhood's hue was mostly determined by the racial makeup of its residents, as well as their occupation and income level.

According to the maps that were included in a government house lending guidebook at the San Leandro Public Library, "incompatible racial groups should not be permitted to live in the same communities." The government thereby denied African Americans insured mortgage loans, which created segregation. As for the architectural styles of San Leandro, they tended to be less progressive than their neighbors to the north in Berkeley and more in keeping with current-day trends. Prior to World War, II the architectural styles in this quiet rural suburb were primarily Victorian, Queen Anne, Tudor, and Craftsman. These ornate styles gave way to more streamlined modern bungalows after World War II. According to San Leandro's chamber of commerce, the population doubled from 1940 to 1950. What follows is a sampling of photographs from the San Leandro Public Library as well as the Library of Congress featuring homes built in San Leandro and photographs taken close to the time they were built, with original features and landscaping and, possibly, the people who lived there.

Here is a row of tiny houses long before tiny houses were trendy. Mr. and Mrs. Tom Dufy, workers in the nearby canning factory, pose for a photograph on the steps of a cottage in housing that was built for employees of San Lorenzo's California Preserving Company. These simple, small structures were designed with practicality in mind, with pitched roofs, simple stairs, and one window in the front; these are identical features of all of these small temporary homes. (Courtesy San Leandro Public Library and San Leandro History Museum.)

This farmhouse, built before the Craftsman style, was likely constructed with local materials. "Farmhouse" is not necessarily a style of home but is more related to function. This classic and basic early-1900s farmhouse was probably one of the earlier permanent structures in San Leandro and was built to be practical and functional, having very few decorative architectural features on its exterior. This home could also be said to be "prairie style" (Courtesy San Leandro History Museum.)

This is an example of a very basic Free Classic Victorian. It has features that are both Craftsman-like and Victorian. The bay window and ornate details lean towards the Victorian style, while the window designs and columns seem more Craftsman-like. Note that the columns on this house are the same as the 1920s farmhouse, and the window framing is similar to later bungalows. (Courtesy San Leandro Public Library and San Leandro History Museum.)

A family stands in front of their San Leandro home. A white picket fence surrounds the house with a lovely but simple bay window. This home features a pyramid roofline with a pyramid dormer window in the center. The house is obscured by large, bold landscaping, which was popular at the time, and is sided with wooden planks. (Courtesy San Leandro Public Library and San Leandro History Museum.)

This house on Oakes Street in San Leandro is a very typical 1920s bungalow home. It has all the common features of a basic 1920s Craftsman: low-pitched double gable roods, overhanging eaves with exposed beams, patterned window panes, and a covered front porch with bungalow columns. This house features arch details on the front porch. (Courtesy San Leandro Public Library and San Leandro History Museum.)

It is hard to make out the details behind the large, bold landscaping, but this home features a side-by-side double-pitched roof and a covered porch with a striped awning. This was a larger, more stately home that had a tennis court in the back. This home was torn down in 1969, and the site became a fire engine house. (Courtesy San Leandro Public Library and San Leandro History Museum.)

A young boy stands proudly on a street where homes are being built. Note the freshly tilled dirt next to the newer sidewalks. The trees appear to be growing directly in the streets. Empty lots between housing will soon be filled with new modern homes. (Courtesy San Leandro Public Library and San Leandro History Museum.)

Tom Xavier Washington Ave. Between William St. & Ross Ave., 1922.

Trees line Estudillo Street, obscuring homes and creating beautiful shade. The size of the trees indicates that this neighborhood has been established for a while. The homes appear to be Edwardian and Victorian in style with arched windows and decorative features. The setbacks are even, and the stairs to each home are aligned in this clearly well-planned neighborhood. (Courtesy San Leandro Public Library and San Leandro History Museum.)

This photograph showcases a real estate office in a lovely shingle home built in the early 1920s featuring plenty of greenery on the porch and in the landscaping. Note that the stairs were built without rails and that the porch has no rails either. The foundation is a crawl space with very little room to grow, and lattice work wood protects the underside of the home from rodents. Homes built in the early 1920s were generally modest in size. (Courtesy San Leandro Public Library and San Leandro History Museum.)

Ornate features abound on this home that has Victorian, Spanish Revival, and Mission styling all rolled into one. The ornate covered porch, the bold dormer window with Mission styling, and the tiled roof come together as a display of affluence and personal style. The half-circular pop-out on the left with arched windows is absolutely exquisite and a sign of great wealth and taste. (Courtesy San Leandro Public Library and San Leandro History Museum.)

This flyer from the early 1920s advertises the Broadmoor Park neighborhood: "In a large, rapidly growing city, it is seldom possible to be sure of congenial neighbors. You cannot select your own. But in Broadmoor Park this has been done for you. The rigid race, color, and building restrictions placed on the property are your protection." Homes during this era were valued not only for their aesthetic values, but also for the types of people that resided within that community. (Courtesy San Leandro Public Library and San Leandro History Museum.)

Tudor homes were very popular in the early part of the 20th century, characterized by broad, steeply pitched gable roofs, masonry, and stonework and accented with decorative half-timbering. This home features two heavily pitched roofs with a flat-roofed middle portion. The letter "P" is cut out of the exterior shutters; it is likely the first initial of the owner's last name. (Courtesy San Leandro Public Library and San Leandro History Museum.)

A group of men gather to enjoy a feast in the Broadmoor neighborhood of San Leandro in 1939. Judging by the clothing, it appears to be a costume party of some sort. The Broadmoor, one of the oldest neighborhoods in San Leandro, was officially opened in 1908 and annexed by the city of San Leandro. (Courtesy San Leandro Public Library and San Leandro History Museum.)

This is another classic structure in the Queen Anne style mixed with Edwardian features. The scalloped siding along the front is quite decorative, and the pop-out bay window provided a lovely place to sit in the sun and sew or cross stitch or read and socialize. A small covered porch is within the footprint of the house. This would have been a lovely place to call home. (Courtesy San Leandro Public Library and San Leandro History Museum.)

Seen here is a row of tidy little Craftsman bungalows that line this street in San Leandro. The setbacks are all even, the styles of the pitched roofs all march, and the streets have freshly planted trees. Greenery was an essential part of the landscape in the 1920s as it is today. (Courtesy San Leandro Public Library and San Leandro History Museum.)

This is an aerial view of San Leandro featuring Edwardians, Craftsman, and eclectic-style homes and buildings populate the landscape. Plenty of vacant lots are available for future builds, and some of these homes would be torn down to make way for tract housing and modern apartment buildings. (Courtesy San Leandro Public Library and San Leandro History Museum.)

A woman stands outside of her modest Edwardian home at the corner of Carpentier and Hepburn Streets. Note the street names on the picket fence. Edwardian homes are post-Victorians similar to Queen Annes but lacking ornamentation. This home features a multi-gabled roof, simple surfaces and wraparound porches, and a hint of a tower with classical detailing. (Courtesy San Leandro Public Library and San Leandro History Museum.)

Three gentlemen stand in front of a First Bay Tradition (or New Bay) shingle home in San Leandro, next to a fire hydrant. Fires were and still are prevalent in the Bay Area, so hydrants became a modern necessity; invented in Philadelphia in 1801, they were pretty common by the early 20th century. (Courtesy San Leandro Public Library.)

Seen here is classic Victorian styling, obscured by foliage. The ornate pop-out with arched window framing, circler-covered birch, and bay windows are all classic Victorian-era features. It is combined with some Queen Anne features and a hint of Craftsman. The French double doors are a classic feature of this era and were a way of displaying wealth as well as allowing light into the home through stained-glass windows. (Courtesy San Leandro Public Library and San Leandro History Museum.)

This home looks very similar to a Sears catalog home, the Cornell, a classic American Foursquare. A Foursquare is always two stories tall and typically consists of four windows on the front. The roof is hip or pyramid-style, with one dormer popping out from the top. (Courtesy San Leandro Public Library and San Leandro History Museum.)

This home belonged to Mary Brown, San Leandro's first official librarian. On January 31, 1906, the library board of trustees appointed Mary Brown as San Leandro's first official librarian. Her starting salary was $12.50 a month. She served San Leandro from 1906 to 1938. (Courtesy San Leandro Public Library and San Leandro History Museum).

THE CORNELL..
▲ SIX ROOMS AND BATH

MODERN HOME No. 3226B
ALREADY CUT AND FITTED

THIS square American type home is a favorite in suburban areas, as well as in the city where narrow lots predominate. This cozy home with clear bevel siding on the first story walls and clear red Cedar shingles on the second floor, is very economical to build on account of the square lines. A square plan gives the most livable space at the lowest cost. Wide overhanging eaves, well balanced windows and comfortable front porch gives the exterior a substantial appearance.

Quality of Materials Above the Average

"I have been in the building business for more than forty years and have built buildings and homes in several different states and must truly say that your building materials in its several different lines, is second to none. Your delivery is prompt and your business transactions fair and courteous. Since using your material, I figure that I have saved twenty five per cent on each job, besides the satisfaction of receiving grades as specified."

J. W. Bailey,
Dillsboro, Ind.

FIRST FLOOR PLAN

From the front porch you enter the living room size 15 ft. 11 inches by 12 ft. 6 inches. Four large windows admit plenty of light and the good wall space permits many attractive arrangements of the furniture. A closet for outer wraps opens off the stair platform—handy to the front door. The dining room size 11 ft. 3 inches by 12 ft. 2 inches and the kitchen complete the first floor plan. Note the kitchen has cross ventilation and a convenient space for all necessary equipment. The platform at the top of the grade and cellar stairs is designed for refrigerator.

SECOND FLOOR PLAN

The upstairs hall connects the three corner bedrooms and bath. Each room has cross ventilation and the bath is above the average size with built-in linen closet over the main stairs.

WHAT OUR BASE PRICE INCLUDES

At the base price quoted, we will furnish all materials needed to build this six room and bath home consisting of lumber, lath, millwork, flooring, roof shingles, building paper, 24-inch red Cedar shingles with two coats of stain for the second story sidewalls, clear bevel siding for first story, hardware, metal and paint materials according to specifications. All framing material completely ready cut.
Heating, lighting, plumbing and other options shown on the price list.
Select your garage from designs shown on Pages 62 and 63.

SECOND FLOOR PLAN

FIRST FLOOR PLAN

The Cornell by Sears, in the 1930s, is a home similar to the Camacho house. This advertisement from the Sears modern homes catalog of 1936 states, "This square American type home is a favorite in suburban areas, as well as in the city where narrow lots predominate. This cozy home with clear bevel siding on the first-story walls and clear red Cedar shingles on the second floor, is very economical to build on account of the square lines."

A small blurb in the *Oakland Tribune* on February 4, 1923, states that the housing conditions and general sanitation in San Leandro are better than average. Better than average does not seem like a great sales pitch, but for some, this was motivation to move to the newly built suburbs.

A Spanish-tiled roof is next to a more-simple roof likely made of composition shingle or sheathing. Both homes feature exterior decorative shutters and small covered porches—much smaller and more practical of use than the porches of the 1920s which were designed for outdoor socializing. Window framing in the mid-century was more likely to be aluminum framed than wood. (Library of Congress.)

Seen here is a typical San Leandro home with wraparound windows on both sides. The placement of the chimney shows that the fireplace was more toward the middle of those houses. A pop-out window on the side is a lovely place to sit. A detached garage was a common feature. Tidy, clean lines are the emphasis in this modern bungalow. (Library of Congress.)

Here is a row of classic mid-century bungalows with small front porches and tidy yards. Later homes feature more manufactured details, such as the metal railings that were mass-produced. Varying rooflines and facades create variety, while even setbacks make the neighborhood feel neat and tidy. Small trees are planted in a line along the sidewalk. (Library of Congress.)

This row of homes features different styles—one small Spanish revival next to more Tudor-style pitched roofs. The Tudor home would have featured ornate pitched ceilings inside along with a decorative and functional fireplace. Note the individually framed window panes windows of the smaller Spanish-style home along with its ornate tiled roof. (Library of Congress.)

This is a classic San Leandro tract house bungalow from the 1940s with tidy and manicured shrubbery across its modern front. This home is topped with a triple-gable front roof with single-gable side roofing and clean lines throughout. Shutters, awnings, and streamlined details make this the perfect modest postwar home in San Leandro. (Photograph by the author.)

Seen here is a level-in small rancher home with a side gable roof and very clean lines. Classic tract housing was designed for easy modern living. This home features hand-cut decorative shutters on the front and a fireplace between the garage and the main home. A mailbox flap on the right side allows mail carriers to deliver mail directly to the inhabitants—a modern wonder invented in the late 19th century. (Photograph by the author.)

Three

ALAMEDA

Prior to 1864, Alameda was home to a few small farmhouses scattered around the peninsula (and prior to that, it was inhabited by native populations). Things shifted in the 1960s when a rail and ferry system was introduced to the city. In order to create a functional shipping harbor, from 1874 until 1902, the Oakland Estuary was dredged out, which to turned Alameda from a peninsula into an island. With improved transportation, hubs of commerce sprang up along the train routes, and as more commerce appeared, so did more houses. Like most other East Bay cities, Alameda grew by leaps and bounds after the 1906 earthquake and fire in San Francisco.

The Island of Alameda's architecture, much like that of neighboring Oakland, is primarily Craftsman-style homes with many unique and beautiful Craftsman details. Alameda is also well-known for Victorian architecture, but for the purpose of this book, the focus will remain on 20th-century residential architecture. Alameda has many special neighborhoods from Fernside to the West End and Bay Farm, to the floating homes of the marina. It is impossible to touch on everything in one chapter, so this section will instead turn its attention to fun highlights.

Oakland-Alameda Tube #14

The Posey Tube was completed and opened to traffic on October 27, 1928. The ventilation buildings on the exterior of the tube that house the exhaust and fresh air fans were built in an Art Deco style. The tube was designed to bring cars to and from Alameda under the estuary. Without the tunnel, the development of the West End of Alameda would have been greatly hindered. (Courtesy bridgeoftheweek.com)

San Francisco
(Ferry Station, Foot of Market St.)

SOUTHERN PACIFIC LINES

and

Alameda

Ferry and Electric Train Service

Lunch Counter and Table Service on all Ferry Boats   Form 7

Subject to change without notice

The ferry and train brought people from San Francisco and Oakland to Alameda, which encouraged building in the Island City. Ferry boats featured a lunch counter and table service onboard. Wide boulevards, both in Alameda and Oakland, were designed so that both trains and horse-drawn carriages (and later, cars) could share the road. (Courtesy Alameda Museum.)

This very sweet photograph from 1928 features a family preparing to build on a piece of land in Alameda. Behind it is a really interesting home with arches and castle-like features. The siding has not yet been added, and the homes in the background appear to be unfinished also. (Courtesy Bancroft Library, University of California.)

This is a grand residence in Alameda. This spacious home features a complex roof system, wide columns to support the porch (made of brick), and two chimneys. The bay window is an added feature that could be considered another sign of the wealth and style of the family. Exposed beams support the eaves and brick pillars support the roof over the porch. (Courtesy Bancroft Library, University of California.)

RESIDENCE·MR.F.S.LOOP   ALAMEDA

LOT 40x150, NEW MODERN COTTAGE, 7 ROOMS BATH, ETC. $500 CASH; BALANCE, TERMS TO SUIT

This unique Alameda home encompasses many different styles. The advertising postcard states, "New Modern Cottage, 7 Rooms. Bath, Etc. $500 Cash; Balance, Terms To Suit." This home encompasses so many unique features and would be considered eclectic style. A turret, arched windows, a covered porch entry, and stained glass are all part of this beautiful "modern" home. (Courtesy Bancroft Library, University of California.)

A tidy row of bungalows in a variety of styles is an exemplary representation of what one can expect in Alameda. They feature arched doorways, covered porches, decorative awnings, and tidy front lawns. All the homes along the street have the same setback, creating a uniform suburban feel to the neighborhood, while the varied rooflines and facades create variety. (Courtesy Alameda History Museum.)

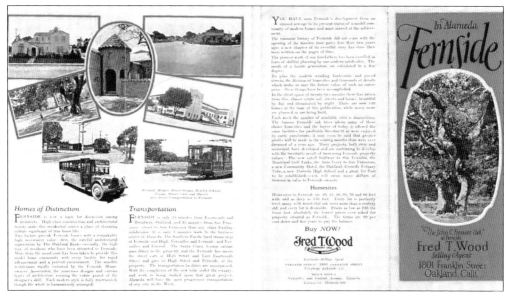

This brochure states, "YOU HAVE seen Fernside's development from an unused acreage to its present status of a model community of modern homes and must marvel at the achievement." The brochure goes on to detail how Fernside came into existence. The brochure exclaims, "Fernside is now a topic for discussion among architects. High class construction and architectural beauty make this residential center a place of charming culture significant of true home life. Two factors provide Fernside homes with a remarkably high investment value—first, the careful architectural supervision by The Oakland Bank—secondly, the high type of residents who have been attracted to Fernside." (Courtesy fernsideHOA.com)

This Fernside cottage is similar in design to the MacGregors, which will be touched on later in the book, but it is also similar to many catalog or plan book homes. The circular entryway with a heavy carved wooden door is unique and in a Storybook style. The front of the house has an arched window and a chimney for the wood-turning fireplace that goes up on the right side of the building. (Photograph by the author.)

This is a page from the Pacific Ready-Cut Homes catalog from the 1920s. Simply known as "style 292," this home arrived shipped via rail freight, ready to assemble—hence the name "Ready-Cut Homes." This home features the curved pitched front gable roof style and an arched doorway, very similar to homes built by local builders here in the Bay Area. (Courtesy archive.org.)

Another classic Fernside home is pictured here, with a curved front gable roof over the small porch and a side gable roof over the main part of the house. The covered porch has a triangular top and an arched doorway beyond that. The gentle slope accentuates the entry and makes the diminutive front porch a feature point of the home. The stairs are made of brick, which gives the entry a quaint village feel. The large picture window in the front allows for plenty of light, and a fireplace on the side of the home provides warmth. (Photograph by the author.)

A classic Alameda bungalow with a wide porch that has an arched overhang, exposed beams, and a modern sleek rectangular shed-style dormer window is seen here. Brick beams and supports hold the porch up, and chains hang around the permitter to keep people from falling off the porch, although probably not very well. (Photograph by the author.)

A very similar home to the one at the top of the page is the Buena Vista: a Wardway home (by Montgomery Ward), except with a pitched roof on the dormer. It came either pre-cut, or one could buy the plans and supplies. "Seldom do you see a more inviting and conformable home than 'The Buena Vista.' The keynote of the whole home, both inside and out, is given by the wide porch with its heavy beams supported by massive columns at both ends." (Courtesy internetarchive.org)

"The Buena Vista"—Material Supplied Either Ready-Cut or Not Ready-Cut

Charming, Popular, Four-Bedroom Bungalow

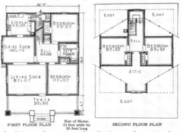

SELDOM do you see a more inviting and comfortable home than "The Buena Vista." The keynote of the whole home, both inside and out, is given by the wide porch with its heavy beams supported by massive columns at both ends, and the broad steps flanked by the stone buttresses, giving an air of comfort and hospitality thoroughly carried out in the plan. The low dormer, with its overhanging roof supported by timber brackets, and the bay window entrance in the dining room, are especially attractive features.

One enters directly into the large living room, and beyond, through the cased opening, is the dining room. Directly opposite the front door a heavy two-panel door leads into the center hall, an arrangement which has enabled the architects to keep every room most accessible, at the same time allowing every room to be isolated if desired. It is unnecessary in this home to pass through one bedroom to reach another or to reach the bathroom—a fault so common in bungalow planning.

Opening into the bathroom there is a linen closet such as is illustrated on Page 51. To the rear of the dining room the light kitchen with twin window over the sink and a third window over the worktable, makes a fine, airy, light workroom for the housewife. The large case is our design No. 863, illustrated on Page 53.

The rear entrance is through the grade door with steps leading down to the cellar and up into the kitchen. This makes a double door into the kitchen, which keeps it warm and cozy in winter.

Upstairs are two fine big bedrooms, each with a big closet, and a large attic for storage space. "The Buena Vista" is a home for a large family or for the small, comfort-loving family who want extra room for their guests.

FIRST FLOOR PLAN   Size of Home,   SECOND FLOOR PLAN
                    31 feet wide by
                    36 feet long

See Prices on Pages 1 to 4—Specifications on Pages 10 and 11

Unless you request otherwise we furnish for this home, Colonial yellow paint for the sidewalls and white for the trim.

See Page 4 for heating equipment, etc., option of Radio Asphalt Shingles and oak flooring and finish. Write us for suggestions and estimates on a water supply system and sewage disposal for this home.

This home features a very steep-pitched roof, a shingled exterior, and a small covered porch that is within the footprint of the house. Two modest Roman Tuscan–style columns support the front porch. A brick chimney rises high above the roofline. Simple clean lines are along the roof line with hidden eaves, and a diamond shape vent provides air to the small triangular attic. (Photograph by the author.)

The roof lines on this house go in every direction, with front and side gables featuring wild exposed beams reaching out from underneath like tentacles. The expansive porch is filled with lush foliage and flanked by wide stone-covered columns. The windows are square in shape but have arched features within the framework. (Courtesy Bancroft Library, University of California.)

A combination of arched and rectangular windows brings light to this eclectic-style home. An angled bay window on the right over the stairs has elements of Victorian homes, while the simple lines lean toward the Edwardian. Shingles along the second floor and wood siding along the first floor give this home a special uniqueness. (Photograph by the author.)

This house has a side gabled roof with a little pop-up shed-style dormer window. The wide columns supporting the fully covered porch are made of stone and have been painted. This is a classic Craftsman in Alameda. A small brick chimney rests on the right-hand side of the roof. Palm trees line the street behind this home, making for a very California-style scene. (Photograph by the author.)

These classic Greek ionic columns support the generous side porch of this elegant home. One dormer window pops out of the top of the pyramid roof style—a divergence from the standard dormer roofs seen on most homes. A faux balcony provides an opulent feel under the two upper bedrooms. The square shape of this home and the porch on the side are all classic Edwardian features. (Photograph by the author.)

This is an eclectic Victorian home featuring a hipped ridge roof with a little pop-out dormer vent. The placement of the windows evokes Edwardian columns. The steep stairs lead up to a small centered entryway with no real porch and a modest Victorian double door. The steps were probably rebuilt later in the 20th century. (Photograph by the author.)

Presently, it seems, everyone loves a spite house, but it has not always been that way. The famous spite house in Alameda is an occupied residence in the East End of Alameda. Back in the 1930s, the city of Alameda took a substantial portion of the land owned by Charles Froling to make way for another street. Froling had planned to build on this land and was not giving up. The Alameda Spite House is 54 feet long and only 10 feet wide.

This photograph caption reads, "Residence of A.V. Clark in Alameda, on Peru Street." A stately mansion of modest size, this house is eclectic with Edwardian, Craftsman, and Victorian features. An arched sculpted design covers the window and is supported by half Tuscan columns in almost an Italian Renaissance relief style. Balconies along the second floor have low railings with detailed balusters that hold up the banister. (Courtesy Bancroft Library, University of California.)

This is another classic Craftsman that has a smaller porch supported by Tuscan columns, with a pyramid roof and shed-style dormer window. Wood shingles and faux shutters cover the front of the home. Note the exposed beams under the roof line across the front of the house, this is the iconic, classic feature of a California Craftsman. (Photograph by the author.)

Pictured is a beautiful large home for sale in Central Alameda. This grand-size house features dormer windows and two chimneys. Note the columns and small porch and shrubbery for privacy. According to the *Oakland Tribune*, on May 3, 1936, "This beautiful home, located at 1639 Dayton Avenue in Alameda, is open for inspection, under the management of E.H. Richardson, Alameda real estate dealer."

IN ALAMEDA

This beautiful home, located at 1639 Dayton Avenue in Alameda, is open for inspection, under the management of E. H. Richardson, Alameda real estate dealer.

This June 28, 1936, *Oakland Tribune* newspaper article offers for sale a lovely Tudor-style Fernside home with a steeply pitched roof, hand-hewn timber siding, and Tudor charm. The advertisement states, "This beautiful home, located at 1429 Gibbons Drive, in Fernside, Alameda, is open for inspection, under the management of Richardson's Alameda Real Estate Dealers. The artistically landscaped grounds, with fountain and patios, are one of the features."

FERNSIDE HOME

This beautiful home, located at 1429 Gibbons Drive, in Fernside, Alameda, is open for inspection, under the management of Richardson's, Alameda real estate dealers. The artistically landscaped grounds, with fountain and patios, are one of the features.

Here is a photograph of a tank house in Alameda's West End. Thousands of similar structures were built in California from the 1850s to the 1930s. These structures are tall and narrow and often behind a house. Tank houses were essentially a simple, small water system supplying homes with water before electricity and municipal water. (Photograph by the author.)

Here is a complex Craftsman featuring an M-shaped dormer on the second floor. Built in 1915, this shingled Craftsman was added onto over the years and lifted to complete a full basement and a third floor. Squared columns support the large front porch designed for socializing. The interior (not shown) features inlaid wooden floors and a gracious but modest staircase. The author and her family sit on the stairs. (Photograph by Alex Vinson.)

Floating homes or houseboats have been a part of Alameda since the dredging of the estuary at the beginning of the 20th century. They are differentiated from houseboats in that they are attached to the land with a fixed and permanent location. They have electricity and sewage pumped in from city sources. (Courtesy Alameda History Museum.)

This home features clean lines and mid-century modern architecture. It has an early-style single-story structure, more like a trailer home on a barge, with a simple rectangular design and a lightweight aluminum and wood siding composition. A flat roof overhangs a small porch with a sliding glass door. (Courtesy Richard Boland.)

The semi-mansard roofline of this house has serious party vibes; slatted windows allow a bay breeze into this cozy two-story floating home. A wide sliding glass door opens onto a front patio. This residence is half boat and half house with a spacious late-1960s design built not on a foundation, but on a floating platform with a permanent dock. (Courtesy Richard Boland.)

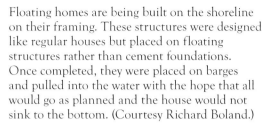

Floating homes are being built on the shoreline on their framing. These structures were designed like regular houses but placed on floating structures rather than cement foundations. Once completed, they were placed on barges and pulled into the water with the hope that all would go as planned and the house would not sink to the bottom. (Courtesy Richard Boland.)

Pictured from left to right, Richard Boland, Leonard Farutto, and Jerry Fruit pose on top of a newly built home on the estuary. Note that the small porch has minimal railings, as this was prior to serious concerns about safety. The roof has wood shingles and a mansard roofline. A wood-framed door with glass panes provides entry to the upper level of this cozy two-bedroom floating paradise. (Courtesy Richard Boland.)

Pictured is the interior of a floating home that features a round fireplace next to a round bed with a Japanese-style screen for privacy. Downstairs is a full living room with an ornate heavy dining set and a mid-century-style living room arrangement. A small galley kitchen is in the back with a full-size stove for cooking and an area for serving up cocktails. (Courtesy Richard Boland.)

Floating Homes Born of Dream

By WILLIAM DOYLE
Tribune Financial Editor

Richard Boland was living in a rented houseboat tied up on the Alameda side of the Oakland Estuary.

One night, lulled by the motion of the water and half asleep, he started thinking about all of the visitors who wanted to know how he liked houseboat life and how they could buy such a home.

He went from the dreamy state to some hard thinking and now, in partnership with a young engineer, is building "floating homes at the Pacific Marina in Alameda.

Boland differentiates between the floating homes which he is building to be tied up at a permanent location and house boats which have power and can move about.

He would also like to differentiate between his floating homes and the arks and other strange craft which have plagued Bay cities periodically.

The youthful entrepreneur intends to do more than wish about that.

He is going to approach the city of Alameda with a request that a uniform code be adopted covering all aspects of floating homes from their construction through locations where they may be moored to requirements for living aboard them. Oakland is on his list after Alameda.

This August 20, 1968, *Oakland Tribune* article tells the story of how floating homes in Alameda grew from an idea into a reality. "He went from the dreamy state to some hard thinking and now, in partnership with a young engineer, is building 'floating homes' at the Pacific Marina in Alameda." Boland also distinguishes his floating homes and the "arks and other strange craft which have plagued Bay cities periodically."

Four

BERKELEY AND ALBANY

Modern Berkeley homes were initially constructed around the newly built College of California (later the University of California) starting in the late 19th century. Like many East Bay towns, the slow, sleepy increase in population shifted dramatically upward with the great earthquake and fire in San Francisco. A variety of sources claim that single-family zoning may have originated in Berkeley in 1916 as part of an effort to keep minorities out of white neighborhoods. Berkeley was developing rapidly during the early part of the 20th century; the population of Berkeley was 40,434 in 1910 and increased to 56,036 in 1920 due to the increased availability of transportation to Oakland and San Francisco. Shortly thereafter, however, a major fire swept through Berkeley destroying 640 structures, which created opportunities for new multifamily developments. Later, Berkeley experienced an additional period of fast development during World War II when large numbers of people moved to the Bay Area to work in war industries, including the Kaiser Shipyards in nearby Richmond.

The most popular home styles built in Berkeley and Albany in the first half of the 20th century are the Mediterranean, influenced by Spanish and Italian styles with tiled roofs, arched features, and large windows. Craftsman bungalows, of course, are also incredibly prevalent and often done with a bit of Mediterranean flare. There are traditional English homes and Tudor homes with steep-pitched gable roofs, hand-hewn half-timbering, masonry, and leaded-glass windows. Brown Shingles are incredibly popular throughout Berkeley and dot the hills in many different styles from cottage to modern.

Berkeley has always been known as a very progressive city, and while for the most part, its architecture is deeply rooted in the early 20th-century Craftsman style, there were also many more advanced and unique style homes. A handful of incredibly inspirational and well-known architects have influenced Berkeley's style, including Bernard Maybeck, Julia Morgan, and Lilian Bridgeman.

Just north of Berkeley with similar architecture and culture is Albany, initially a small suburban hamlet with a population of only 20,000. Interestingly, Albany was originally incorporated as Ocean View after a dispute with Berkeley over the dumping of garbage in 1908. The city then changed its name shortly thereafter to Albany after the birthplace of its first mayor (there were too many other towns called Ocean View). Albany attempted several times to annex to Berkeley but remained independent and its own separate entity.

For anyone familiar with Albany houses, it is likely that they have heard of Charles MacGregor, who was known for having constructed more than 1,500 homes throughout the city (he also built homes all over the East Bay). MacGregor homes, which were primarily built in the 1920s and 1930, were known for fine architectural detailing and split-level living. Bedrooms are frequently located up a small flight of stairs and placed over a garage. The MacGregor classic had a Mediterranean look and featured archways, picture windows, tiled fireplaces, and built-in cabinetry and shelving.

There is so much iconic Berkeley and Albany architecture, and the following is merely a sampling.

North from Hearst below Walnut

The 1923 Berkeley, California, fire destroyed over 600 structures, including 584 houses in the neighborhoods north of the University of California, Berkeley, on September 17, 1923. This led to increased fire safety in buildings and landscapes, as well as clearing the way for more modern housing development. (Courtesy Bancroft Library, University of California.)

Designed by Lilian Bridgeman, this house was meant to fit into the natural environment upon which it was built. Interestingly, this home featured a driveway and attached garage even though automobile culture had not fully developed yet—another way in which this style was visionary. (Courtesy Bancroft Library, University of California.)

This home features elaborately placed wood shingles on its exterior, open eaves, and a balcony overhanging the garage. Very much influential in the Tahoe style that would follow, this home is American Craftsman at its best, with a more rustic styling meant to evoke the surrounding topography. (Courtesy Bancroft Library, University of California.)

The interior of this house has a rustic feel with an exposed beam ceiling and brick fireplace, including a cozy restful place for reading. Two rocking chairs and a wingback chair all face each other in the perfect place for socializing around a warm fire. Flowers are placed on the edge of the mantle to enhance the natural feel of the space. (Courtesy Bancroft Library, University of California.)

Lilian Bridgeman's Davis house is being built. The home is on a downslope with two fireplaces and a pitched angled modern roof. The exterior will be wooden siding, and there is a minimal setback from the road, which provides no front yard, as in more traditional styles. Plenty of windows all around will allow light into the interior. (Courtesy Bancroft Library, University of California.)

Modern open eaves, dark finishes with plenty of windows, and exterior shingle features were influential throughout the rest of the 20th century. Natural, dark-stained wood planks cover the top portion with large brown shingles along the bottom floor, creating a modern feel. Plenty of planned greenery covers the land to accent the natural style of the exterior architecture. (Courtesy Bancroft Library, University of California.)

Every detail down to the smallest window and hand-crafted heavy front door was considered carefully in the building of this home. Thick leaded glass in metal framing provides light with privacy. The heavy wide framing around the door is evocative of the redwoods from which this home was likely crafted. (Courtesy Bancroft Library, University of California.)

A friend of architect Bernard Maybeck, Lilian Bridgeman began her career as a schoolteacher but started a second career at age 44 as an architect. She was a strong woman, indeed. Here, she is in a smock over her dress with her hair pulled up, working on architectural designs. (Courtesy Bancroft Library, University of California.)

Lilian Bridgeman is pictured as a young woman in 1885 prior to her arrival in Berkeley. She was a founding member of the Hillside Club, which promoted more rustic architecture and set out to enhance the natural setting of Berkeley's North Side. She was very influential in Berkeley's early architecture and design as well as throughout the Bay Area. (Courtesy Bancroft Library, University of California.)

Spanish tiles and modern clean lines mix in this hillside home. Like many hill homes, this house takes advantage of elevated topography to create a unique and spacious multilevel home. This house features archways, balconies, and a path down the hillside to take the homeowner back to nature. (Courtesy Bancroft Library, University of California.)

This eclectic and expansive home is surrounded by foliage, trees, and greenery. It is a multilevel home built into a hill with a complex stair system and patios and a sideways Spanish-tiled gable roof. Arched doorways under the stairs and wooden columns are additional unique features. (Courtesy Bancroft Library, University of California.)

Two women stand in the shaded staircase of the Stevenson home. The double-door screened entry to the lower level and upper level are perfectly designed with three panes, three hinges, and a small knob. The porch is framed and supported with columns. (Courtesy Bancroft Library, University of California.)

A man enjoys some leisure time next to a warm fireplace and attractive ornamented arched doorway. A built-in bookshelf is topped with a tiled opening for decorative items. Hardwood floors meet a brick hearth at the fireplace. Built-in electric sconce lighting and light switches were still relatively new features in this "modern" home. (Courtesy Bancroft Library, University of California.)

The home is surrounded by trees and what appears to be a fruit orchard along a rolling hill. It is painted a white color with Spanish-tiled roofing supported by wooden beams. Wood-framed windows open with hinges (rather than sliding up and down), and a small balcony overlooks the side of the house and the back. (Courtesy Bancroft Library, University of California.)

Seen here is a typical large First Bay Tradition shingle home in Berkeley, perched on a hill. Three ladies and one gentleman stand outside under the imposing ivy that flanks the front exterior. A bay window on the right side overlooks the hillside. The pyramid roof has simple lines without exposed eaves, giving it a more streamlined appearance compared to a Craftsman-style home. (Courtesy Bancroft Library, University of California.)

A showcase of four homes in Berkeley appeared in a June 1926 article in the *San Francisco Chronicle*. The article states, "These four charming homes just finished in Thousand Oaks Heights, Berkeley, are examples of the high type of architecture being displayed. They are of Spanish, English and Queen Anne English style."

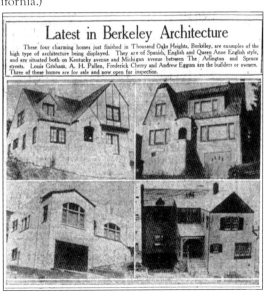

Similar in design to a classic Foursquare, this First Bay Tradition shingle home features plenty of windows for a bright interior, natural redwood shingles, exposed dark-colored eaves, and plenty of pop-out windows to make the exterior more intricate and interesting. This house was featured in an early 2000s *San Francisco Chronicle* article on Arts and Crafts architecture and was designed by Leona Hall. (Photograph by the author.)

Pictured is the quintessential Berkeley Bungalow with a double-pitched roof. It is most likely that the porch was enclosed after this home was built, but it is also possible that it was built with an enclosed porch. Built in 1921, the interior had a breakfast nook and many fine wood details. (Photograph by the author.)

An early Albany home with a steeply pitched roof offers one small window to allow light into the second floor, likely where the bedrooms are. Larger windows on the lower floor allow for more light. A woman and child sit behind the picket fence on the porch steps. Note the sign that says, "House for Sale." (Courtesy the Albany Library Historical Collection.)

This is a classic Bay Area Craftsman with exposed beams, a pitched roof, and low dormer windows. The porch is not covered, which is unusual for this era of construction. Note the brick chimney on one side that goes up and through the eave on the roofline. Brick columns flank either side of the front, and siding along the bottom is an interesting touch. The aluminum-framed windows indicate that this photograph was taken in the 1950s or later. (Courtesy the Albany Library Historical Collection.)

A family stands in front of this unique home in Albany farmlands. The roof style of this house is notable, with a center steep-pitched gable roof. The bottom portion of the house is stuccoed, while the top has redwood shingles. An enclosed porch on the back appears to slope toward the backyard, which would allow water from clothes washing to drain off the back. A very close look reveals that there are three children, two baby dolls, and one small pup in the image. (Courtesy the Albany Library Historical Collection.)

Here is that same house about 40 years later—the porch has been enclosed and the exterior of the home stuccoed. The rolling hills of farmland have been divided up into lots and a street and sidewalk have been laid out in front. The architectural features, except the shingles, remain about the same, however. (Courtesy the Albany Library Historical Collection.)

This is a classic California Craftsman bungalow with an arched entry, covered porch, and bay window. Complex roofing system with multilevel eaves and some Spanish tile over the rounded bay window on the left. The house features a well-manicured front lawn and what appears to be a fenced-in backyard. Two young girls sit on the sides of the stairs. (Courtesy the Albany Library Historical Collection.)

This house looks like a plan book or flat pack home; however, there were no similar corresponding images from any of the major catalog manufacturers. This could be the view of the rear of the home with a patio on the other side. The dormer window at the top is almost standard issue for homes of this period. (Courtesy the Albany Library Historical Collection.)

Years later, this same home was put up for sale after having been updated with siding and new trim. The picket fence was removed, and a more-decorative railing was added along with a brick retaining wall at the base. Additionally, it appears as though the basement was finished later. (Courtesy the Albany Library Historical Collection.)

Charming Pomona Avenue Homes

Views showing some of the clever artistic homes built by G. W. Owens, Owens Building and Engineering Company, on Pomona avenue near Marin avenue. A living room interior, as furnished by John Breuner Company, is also shown.

This New Albany development was advertised in the *San Francisco Chronicle*. These homes were built by G.W. Owens and are described as "clever" and "artistic." They featured arched entryways, paned windows, and a mixture of roofing styles integrating flat roofs, Spanish-tile detailing, and some pitched and arched features. Awnings are an added decorative and functional ornamentation. (Courtesy *Oakland Tribune*, June 14, 1925.)

This classic MacGregor-style home features a unique pitched roof style and a classic split level with the bedrooms over the attached garage. Constructed mostly during the 1920s and 1930s, MacGregor homes are known for unique architectural stylings such as this and a split-level design. (Photograph by the author.)

WORKINGMEN'S BUNGALOWS

This Mediterranean version served as the heir of the Mission Revival's sunny California image

This small stucco bungalow is typical of houses developed all over California in the 1920s and '30s — the opposite end of the scale from the contemporaneous Period Revival palaces like the Hume Cloister.

The Mediterranean version of these little houses was the most common, with red tile roofs, white or pastel stucco walls, and round arches on the porch and the big front "studio" window. Since these features were essentially a facade applied to a plain, rectangular, flat-roofed cottage, other period styles — medieval farmhouses, castles, pueblos — could be fashioned just as easily, and were. But the

Mediterranean led in popularity for these as it did for the Spanish Colonial mansions of the day, as the heir of the Mission Revival's sunny California image.

The Mediterranean bungalow shown here on Park Stret in southwest Berkeley dates from 1932. In contrast to the whole streets of such houses developed by C. M. MacGregor and other builders in Albany, East Oakland and flatlands Berkeley, this was a later infill in an older neighborhood, the San Pablo Park tract subdivided by Mason-McDuffie in 1906.

Though San Pablo Park has a few rows of identical houses built speculatively, it was a tract of the early 20th century type, where the developer provided the lots and amenities, and the purchasers built their own homes. Bounded by Derby, Russell and Sacramento streets and San Pablo Avenue, it was laid out in lots 35 feet by 100 feet and aimed at families of modest incomes. Building permits

Small stucco bungalow on 2815 Park St.

Touted as "workingmen's bungalows," these homes featured high style and quality in a small but attractive package. This *Berkeley Gazette* July 13, 1983, article states that "the Mediterranean version of these little houses was the most common, with red tile roofs, white or pastel stucco walls, and round arches on the porch and the big front 'studio' window. Since these features were essentially facade applied to a plain, rectangular, flat-roofed cottage, other period styles—medieval farmhouses, castles, pueblos—could be fashioned just as easily, and were."

This May 25, 1980, *Berkeley Gazette* article looks at what it is like "inside a MacGregor home." People have been fascinated with this mass builder since he started building at the beginning of the 20th century. This article states that MacGregor was considered to be "foolhardy" for building in the undeveloped land of North Berkeley. "It was these jealous competitors who pinned the unworthy nickname of One Nail MacGregor upon him."

The interior of the author's Charles MacGregor home in Albany

Berkeley's Architectural Heritage

Inside a MacGregor home

BERKELEY — The MacGregor Home — it comes in all sizes: small, medium, large and very large. From North Oakland, Berkeley, Albany to El Cerrito, Charles M. MacGregor, beginning in 1897 until the day he died in 1954, built houses by the thousands — houses for people to live in. MacGregor was "people-oriented" in many ways: for the future occupants of his houses he thought of a real home; with his workmen, although stern, he was understanding. His architectural style is predominantly Spanish revival which would have pleased the Peralta family upon whose huge San Antonio Spanish land grant he was building.

Although there are many MacGregor homes in Berkeley, in the 1930s he concentrated building in Albany — more than 1,600 houses. At that time he was considered by his competitors to be foolhardy building in the undeveloped land north of Berkeley. It was these jealous competitors who pinned the unworthy nickname of "One-Nail MacGregor" upon him. His homes are solidly built and timeless. He worked closely with his architect, George Henry Caig, and with all his workers, supervising every detail in order to impart an individuality to every house.

one on Evelyn Street shown here. Although the floor plan is practically the same for each small home, there is always some difference, perhaps only in the shape of the big front window or the location of the livingroom fireplace. There are four rooms, a laundry and a bath. There are two windows in the livingroom and one large window each in the kitchen, diningroom and bedroom (this is one of MacGregor's chracteristics). The entrance is always on the side of the small house, midway up the driveway. Another remarkable feature of the small house is the large livingroom, which takes up almost half the house, from the front hall to the front of the house. The white stucco exterior and tile roof maintain the Spanish appearance.

The large livingroom with the graceful archway from the hall and the high vaulted ceiling lends much to the Mexican decor of our sample home (that of Frances Cheney Lozier). Mexican pottery and plants, sombreros and baskets add to the decor. The diningroom is relatively small with the one large window. A unique feature is the built-in cupboard. Mrs. Lozier's dining room has a Mexican cupboard full of Mexican pottery dishes and a display table with more Mexican curiosadades.

75

Pictured here is a classic MacGregor with a front-facing arched sloped gable roof and a side gable in the back. This split-level house has bedrooms over the attached garage. An enclosed, covered small porch greets visitors at the entryway. These attached garages were smaller than those that were built later in the 20th century for large automobiles. (Photograph by the author.)

This is a view from the hills of recently built bungalow Craftsman homes in Albany. Note that there are plenty of empty lots ready for building in the recently laid streets. Along the front of the photograph are three small bungalow homes. Utility piles are in, but few wires are seen in this photograph. (Courtesy the Albany Library Historical Collection.)

Five

RICHMOND WAR HOUSING

During World War II, there was a frenzy of building all over the East Bay to provide accommodations for workers in the war effort, primarily in Richmond and Alameda with a few offshoots in Albany and El Cerrito. Throughout Richmond, the sound of pounding hammers and buzzing saws could be heard all day long during the early war years. In June 1942, Richmond was a peaceful open landscape of gentle rolling hills and fields and marshes. By January the following year, every lot was covered in wartime housing. Some were multistory apartments, some were small duplexes, and some were family housing and small, single-family homes.

The physical transformation of Richmond was epic. To say Richmond's population increased dramatically is not even close to capturing the spirit of the transformation—from 23,600 people in 1940 to over 93,700 in 1943. During the war, tens of thousands of new residents, white and black, migrated from the economically depressed South and Southwest to work in the shipyards. Richmond was by far the largest war housing development in the Bay.

The architecture is unique and practical, quickly built and hastily planned although with great care and thoughtfulness. While much of this new and temporary population was housed in temporary structures such as demountable, dormitories, and tents, many of these so-called "temporary" units remain today.

Most wartime housing was torn down after the war, but some, such as Atchison Village, were converted to cooperative housing. After the war, so many people—especially African Americans—wanted to stay in the Bay Area. The climate is pleasant, and the Bay Area offered a pleasant change from the Jim Crow racism of the South for a more subtle brand. One community offered an opportunity of "housing for everyone," which people —including White people— thought was a great idea; it was fully integrated housing, but none of them actually wanted to buy there or live there.

In August 1942, Much of Richmond was a vast expanse of empty, sandy rolling hills with very little development. This photo, by the US Housing Authority for the Defense Housing Project, shows the beginning of the building of homes in the flat areas below the rolling hills of Richmond. (Courtesy Richmond History Museum.)

A few months later, in November 1943, it rapidly shifted into a bustling growing community filled with sturdy, practical small homes and large apartment complexes designed and built quickly for the growing population. These homes were practical with flat sloped roofs, simple ventilation systems, and long balconies that ran the length of the building, like motels. (Courtesy Richmond History Museum.)

ROUSSEAU STARTS VAST WAR HOUSING PROJECT

The first of 6000 new shipyard workers' family apartments to be built in Richmond on Cutting Boulevard, between First and Sixteenth and Ohio Streets, are shown here. Oliver M. Rousseau, who has built much of Richmond's war housing this year, has been awarded the construction of 2400 apartments, or $5,000,000 of the new U.S. Maritime Commission's $13,-000,000 war housing project. Shipyard worker families are already moving into some of the newly completed units.

This December 13, 1942, article in the *Oakland Tribune* is headlined "Rousseau Starts Vast War Housing Project." Millions of dollars in taxpayer money were poured into construction in Richmond, California. The article states, "The first of 6000 new shipyard workers' family apartments to be built in Richmond on Cutting Boulevard, between First and Sixteenth and Ohio Streets, are shown here. Oliver M. Rousseau, who has built much of Richmond's war housing this year, has been awarded the construction of 2400 apartments, or $5,000,000 of the new U.S. Maritime Commission's $13,-000,000 war housing project. Shipyard worker families are already moving into some of the newly completed units."

This is a c. 1943 aerial view of Richmond. Streets were laid out in anticipation of the building of war housing to accommodate the needs of the growing population arriving to work in the shipyards of Richmond. People came from all over the United States, but especially from the economically depressed areas of the South, to find opportunities in war work. (Courtesy Richmond History Museum.)

WAR APARTMENTS PROJECT CAL-4176
SEPTEMBER 15 1942   LOOKING NORTHEAST   PHOTOGRAPH NO. 1-830-2
U. S. HOUSING AUTHORITY, CITY OF RICHMOND—DEFENSE HOUSING PROJECT

Apartment buildings were built in days and weeks instead of months and years. Note the lack of power lines, streets, telephone lines, or any signs of infrastructure. Homes were built with simple features, flat roofs, and the most basic amenities. It appears, however, from the photographs that these were built of sturdy redwood, a limited but seemingly abundant resource at the time. (Courtesy Richmond History Museum.)

This is a close-up of government-built war housing. Note the architectural features of a pitched roof, wood-framed windows, and vented skirting around the bottom of the house. While built hastily, the homes were high in quality and construction. Power lines were in, and there were even street lights. (Courtesy Richmond History Museum.)

In this photograph by Ellis Myers, a family relaxes on the lawn outside a public housing development. Simple wood-plank siding, sliding windows, and wood-framed doors adorn the front of these pragmatic buildings. The address printed on the building says 407 West Virginia. Apartment homes were built in rows, and neighborhoods were segregated by race. (Courtesy Richmond History Museum.)

In this image captured by Ellis Myers, a young family wears their Sunday best inside a home in Richmond. The window features layers of rolling blinds, shears, and floral curtains. The floor is wooden. A young mother holds her baby next to her husband with a record player/radio open in the background. (Courtesy Richmond History Museum.)

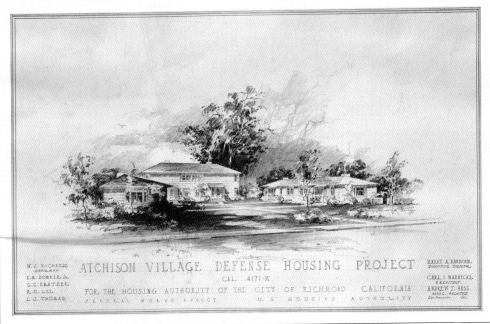

Seen here are 1941 plans for the Atchison Village Defense Housing Project for the Housing Authority of Richmond funded by the US Housing Authority. Atchison Village was a series of apartment homes that were simple with wood-framing, low-pitched roofs, and small front porches with broad, sweeping flat front lawns and small backyards. (Courtesy Richmond History Museum.)

BID OPENING FOR ATCHISON VILLAGE—CAL 4171X, SEPTEMBER 23, 1941, AT OFFICES OF
HOUSING AUTHORITY OF THE CITY OF RICHMOND, CALIFORNIA

People (mostly men) sit around a conference table at the bid opening for Atchison Village Defense Housing Project on September 23, 1941, in Richmond, California. Atchison Village became one of the Bay Area's only cooperative housing complexes having been converted to private use after the war. The blinds are drawn. (Courtesy Richmond History Museum.)

This photograph shows the groundbreaking at Atchison Village. A sign in the background on top of the small office building says, "Louis C. Dunn, General Contractor." One tree shades the office, and a long fence stretches across the property line. Stakes have been placed likely as part of a survey for where the building will be. (Courtesy Richmond History Museum.)

"ATCHISON VILLAGE" CAL 4171X
JANUARY 5, 1942   LOOKING SOUTHWEST FROM STATION NO. 1   NEGATIVE NO. 20
HOUSING AUTHORITY CITY OF RICHMOND—DEFENSE HOUSING PROJECT

This photograph features Atchison Village as it was being built. Some buildings are two-story townhouses, and some are smaller single-level duplexes. The single-story buildings feature bay windows. The automobiles of the builders working on the project line the streets, and utility poles have been placed, bringing modern power to these structures. (Courtesy Richmond History Museum.)

Atchison Village is seen in this view looking south. Power lines have been laid, and the homes are practical but stylish and pleasant. Front porches have not yet been added, and the ground is muddy. Each house has a vent chimney for exhaust, pitched hip roofs with composition shingles, and sliding wood-framed windows. (Courtesy Richmond History Museum.)

"ATCHISON VILLAGE" CAL 4171X
FEBRUARY 6, 1942   LOOKING SOUTH FROM STATION NO. 1   NEGATIVE NO. 26
HOUSING AUTHORITY CITY OF RICHMOND—DEFENSE HOUSING PROJECT

Atchison Village was quickly ready for people to move in. In this photograph, a few workers remain on the lawn doing some landscaping. Lawns have been seeded, covered porches have been added, and trees have been planted. Long, narrow walkways bring new residents from the street to their front doors. (Courtesy Richmond History Museum.)

Here is another project from 1942. A small land bridge over a conduit takes one to endless rows of single-story flat apartment duplexes. One large older home with a mansard roof and dormer windows remains on the right side of the photograph. Power lines stretch as long and far as the eye can see. (Courtesy Richmond History Museum.)

This is an early photograph of Triangle Court from October 1942. Note that the streets are not yet completed, but the houses are on their way. Each duplex home features a chimney in each unit to provide heat from a wood-burning fireplace. There are plenty of windows to provide light. These homes have simple construction, featuring pitched roofs and simple wood siding. (Courtesy Richmond History Museum.)

This photograph shows an artist's vision of what would become Triangle Court. The homes are streamlined, white, and futuristic. This was considered to be a "low rent housing project" built by the Housing Authority of the City of Richmond and was designed by Keith O. Narbett, E. Geoffrey Bangs, and Lester Hurd in 1942. (Courtesy Richmond History Museum.)

Here is a sample design for a home in Triangle Court. The fence is crafted for ivy growth to the left of the entryway, which creates a sense of privacy for the neighboring apartment dweller. Corner windows have two faces in perpendicular directions, allowing light and air to enter a room in two different directions. (Courtesy Richmond History Museum.)

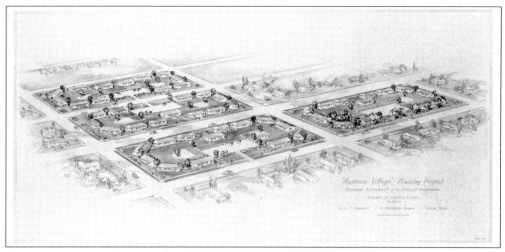

This is a c. 1942 rendering of the Nystrom Village housing project. In the plans for this village, single-level homes surround a central courtyard with a parking lot in the middle. Expansive green lawns surround the homes along with trees. Basic pitched-roof styles with both hip and gable roofs top these homes in various shapes and sizes. (Courtesy Richmond History Museum.)

Here is a photograph featuring Nystrom Village, located at the corner of Maine Avenue and Sixth Street. These were freshly built, stark-white duplex homes with wood-framed paned windows on a crawl-space structure with venting built into the wood siding. Each unit in the duplex has its own wood-burning fireplace, as evidenced by the chimneys. (Courtesy Richmond History Museum.)

A long, flat dusty road stretches across the landscape where new war houses dot the landscape. The white paint on the houses is not quite yet completed. Each home has a little variety with doors on the center, doors on the outer edges, and some appear to have side doors. (Courtesy Richmond History Museum.)

This photograph is captioned "Looking Northeast from Station No. 2" (August 3, 1942). These little duplexes in Nystrom Village have flat roofs and simple vents popping out for ventilation (which indicates that they are piped for gas for cooking and heat). Long, narrow windows adorn the front, and a small privacy screen stands between each front door. (Courtesy Richmond History Museum.).

APRIL 10, 1945   PHOTOGRAPH NO. 8983-3

Community Building No. 119
Project CAL-4416

Looking Northeast from corner of 6th and Maine Streets

F.P.H.A. Housing Authority, City of Richmond
Richmond, California

Workers walk home to their simply designed homes along Sixth Street toward Maine Avenue in Richmond. Older homes in the background have chipping paint and are worn with tall pitched roofs. An old rickety garage in the background harkens back to how Richmond looked before the war. Newer war housing is featured on the right side. An ad for Coca-Cola appears on a billboard in the back. (Courtesy Richmond History Museum.)

After the war, the government put great effort into converting wartime communities into permanent housing for families. Easter Village was a community that welcomed all after the war. Cars are parked outside each fenced-in covered front porch. These two-story townhomes had plenty of light and were designed to be affordable. In the photograph, children play in the foreground while a woman stands on her porch in an apron in the background. (Courtesy Richmond History Museum.)

EPILOGUE

The reader has taken a journey in sampling the various types of Bay Area architecture in the first parts of the 20th century. Not all of it could be touched upon, but this book has highlighted some of the types of homes that make the neighborhoods distinctly of the area and unique while reflecting various times, cultures, and movements in American history.

After the early homes came the ranches and mid-century modern homes. Mid-century modern can be defined as a design movement in interior, products, graphics, architecture, and urban development popular in Western culture from about 1944 to 1970. While the bulk of the East Bay was built up prior to 1944, the mid-century moderns in the East Bay bring culture and character, with designs centered on simplicity and integration with nature. Mid-century architecture ranges from the absolutely mundane tract housing American Dream ranch to the absurd and wild, built with imagination and vision. Mid-century-style homes, like the Craftsmans before them, were a rebellion against the previous ornate styles.

Ranch-style homes, on the other hand, often have mid-century modern features but more traditional rooflines and external details, such as shutters and ordinary paned windows. Pared down, streamlined, and simple, these homes reflected the new modern values of the space age.

Here is a spacious two-story suburban dream home with shutters across the top, a covered porch, and a pitched roof. Clean lines on the side pitch roof meet an attached garage on the right side. This home surely featured a generous floor plan with common areas designed for dining and entertaining and a family space or game room in the back. (Courtesy Sam Benson.)

This is a tidy suburban home with a complex roofing design. A combination of T1-11 siding and bricks cover the front. Faux shutters and a metal gate provide additional character. Distinctively 1960s wood shingles cover the roof. A finely manicured lawn finished off the aesthetic of this classic suburban-style home. This home is on a design spectrum somewhere between classic ranch and mid-century modern. T1-11 is one of the more common types of siding used residentially. It was popular during the 1960s and 1970s because it was inexpensive, light, easy to install, and had a natural wood grain appearance, which was on-trend at the time. (Courtesy Sam Benson.)

2863 San Antonio D[
$42,950   4/2

The common ranch is a postwar modern architectural design in its simplest form. Crafted with a conservative mindset and simple taste, this spacious suburban-style ranch features an attached two-car garage on one side and plenty of windows along the front side. Note that there is some scalloping along the pitched roof on the right side. Faux shutters flank the windows. (Courtesy Sam Benson.)

This long and wide ranch-style house has a wide angled side gabled roof and a spacious attached garage designed for the larger cars of the 1960s. This home has some Craftsman-like features, such as the exposed beams and arched entryway in a Spanish style. Plenty of landscaping covers the front of the house for privacy. This is an attractive, spacious suburban home. (Courtesy Sam Benson.)

This house features a brick fireplace centered under the gabled roof. Addition brick adornment is featured in the columns that support the roof over a small side patio. The home features the modern required feature of an attached garage. There are plenty of windows across the front for light and air, with the upper windows extending all the way to the roofline. The interior featured exposed beams and a spacious open kitchen, dining room, and living room. (Courtesy Sam Benson.)

This is a modest Eichler design listed for sale in the late 1960s. In classic Eichler form, this home features a wide, low-pitched gable roof, a two-car garage, and an entrance on the side. It is interesting to note that none of these more suburban, spacious single-story houses, whether they are mid-century in design or simple ranches, have wide front porches designed for socializing. (Courtesy Sam Benson.)

Seen here is an early advertisement for an Eichler home. Broad, sweeping windows bring the outside in. Bright lighting and a sloped roof with exposed beams have a manufactured home vibe. An open floor plan for a family room, kitchen, and dining area all in one grand space makes this feel modern and spacious in spite of its modest size. (Courtesy internetarchive.org.)

This advertisement from the *Oakland Tribune* on June 3, 1960, states that Eichler homes are "the winner of more awards than any other home in the WORLD. First CHOICE of the American Institute of Architects." There were multiple floor plans and an inner court "open to the sky." The choices in finishes were up to the individual buyer; whether one wanted mahogany paneling floors and cabinet choices, they could choose their own personal color scheme.

The wide-open interior of an Eichler-designed home has high open-beam ceilings (this one was painted white at some point), a central fireplace, and an open floor plan. Eichler homes oozed atomic-era charm and practicality. Bright sunshine fills the great room from the large, wide, and tall plate-glass windows. (Courtesy Sam Benson.)

This spacious Eichler home features a pitched roof in the middle section and a flat roof on the left and right. The house has wood siding along the front and skylights on the top. This home would have featured a bright, natural atrium space in the entryway with an open floor plan throughout. This house has modern, clean lines and plenty of windows in the back for light while providing a sense of privacy. (Courtesy Sam Benson.)

An A-frame house features a steeply angled roofline that begins near, if not at, the foundation line. This design allows for much cheaper construction, as the house is made mostly of roof and windows without all that hullabaloo of walls that other houses require. The post–World War II rise in popularity of the A-frame design is related to its unique modern shape, its inexpensive construction, and the increase in disposable income, which led to many people purchasing vacation homes during the middle of the 20th century. A-frames are often designed to fit into a wooded environment with plenty of windows and light and open floor plans. (Photograph by Milo W. Smith.)

Here is an iconic round house in Oakland designed in 1967 by architect Leon Meyers. A folded plate-style roof tops off this rounded two-bedroom home perched on a hillside in the East Bay. Meyer, an engineer before he became an architect, built a few round houses in the East Bay in the 1960s and 1970s on lots that were otherwise unbuildable. The house was manufactured in a warehouse in pieces and then built on its hillside lot. (Photograph by Milo W. Smith.)

Discover Thousands of Local History Books Featuring Millions of Vintage Images

Arcadia Publishing, the leading local history publisher in the United States, is committed to making history accessible and meaningful through publishing books that celebrate and preserve the heritage of America's people and places.

Find more books like this at
www.arcadiapublishing.com

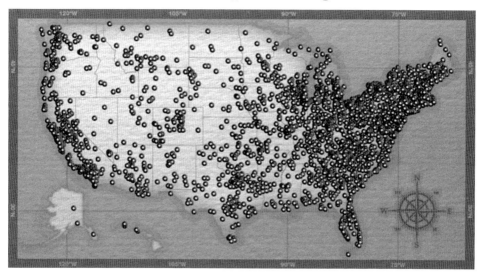

Search for your hometown history, your old stomping grounds, and even your favorite sports team.

Consistent with our mission to preserve history on a local level, this book was printed in South Carolina on American-made paper and manufactured entirely in the United States. Products carrying the accredited Forest Stewardship Council (FSC) label are printed on 100 percent FSC-certified paper.

MADE IN THE USA